Communication
Secrets

The experts tell all!

About the author
Carolyn Boyes MA (Hons),
DCH has been a trainer and
coach for over a decade.
She is the author of *Career
Management*, also in the
business secrets series, and
other books published by
Harper-Collins, including *Cool
Careers, Need to Know? NLP*
and *Need to Know? Cognitive
Behavioural Therapy*.

Communication
secrets

Collins

A division of HarperCollins*Publishers*

77-85 Fulham Palace Road, London W6 8JB

www.BusinessSecrets.net

First published in Great Britain in 2010 by HarperCollins*Publishers*
Published in Canada by HarperCollins*Canada*. www.harpercollins.ca
Published in Australia by HarperCollins*Australia*. www.harpercollins.com.au
Published in India by HarperCollins*PublishersIndia*. www.harpercollins.co.in

1

Copyright © HarperCollins*Publishers* 2010

Carolyn Boyes asserts the moral right to be identified as the author of this work.

A catalogue record for this book is available from the British Library.

ISBN 978-0-00-732444-6

Printed and bound at Clays Ltd, St Ives plc

Contents

Communicate effectively in business

Communication is at the heart of everything we do in business, yet poor communication is a huge problem for businesses and individuals, causing low morale, poor performance and high staff turnover. Much communication happens by accident, with the wrong messages coming across. If you want to be successful in business, it is worth learning about really good communication.

As a person working in international business throughout my career, I have seen how communication can help and hinder relationships within an organization, and impact on teams and goals for the business as a whole. Poor communication can cause stress and hardship for individuals within an organization.

With a background in languages and sales, I have always found words extremely important to me. People in business can earn big money from being skilled with words but can also lose their jobs if they have poor communication skills. Communication can often be distorted because people think they have said one thing but have really given a totally different message. During the last 10 years, as trainer of Neuro-Linguistic Programming, I have become aware of the deeper communication that goes on between individuals and groups through non-verbal communication. That's why it's important that all business people consider the secrets of communication.

This book consists of 50 **secrets** in total, divided into seven chapters.

■ **Firm foundations.** Shows you the essentials of communication you can take into any situation.

■ **Body basics.** Explains non-verbal communication and what to look out for.

■ **Team talk.** Gives you the run-down on communicating with your colleagues or your boss.

■ **Making the most of meetings.** Tells you what to do in a meeting or presentation.

■ **Selling successfully.** Gives you the secrets of how you can communicate effectively with clients.

■ **Dealing at a distance.** Helps you with the ins and outs of telephone calls and emails.

■ **Ditching the difficulties.** Puts you in charge of difficult communication situations.

Do not take good communication for granted, but rather plan and practise your communication skills.

Firm
foundations

Pay attention to the fundamentals of communication to get your message across in the way you want to, both for yourself and for your business. With good communication, you will avoid being misunderstood and expressing inconsistent or unclear messages, ideas, feelings and instructions. Instead, you will become more effective in your career and form stronger relationships with both colleagues and clients.

1.1

Take responsibility

Yes, it sounds basic, but most of us just open our mouths and speak without prior thought. Yet, whether you are talking or just standing around, you are communicating. So take responsibility. Everything you say and do gives a message in business about how you see yourself and your job.

It is said that we:

"Hear half of what is said; listen to half of that; understand half of that; believe half of that, and remember half of that." **(Anon)**

Face to face or on the telephone, business is won and lost by communication. If you don't communicate well enough to a customer or to your boss, you might lose money or your next promotion. The real communication is the message the other person picks up. Take these steps to make sure you always are in control of your message.

one minute wonder One of the first steps you can take to improve your communication is to make it two-way. Sometimes you need to hold back from telling others about all the wonderful things you know and start listening instead.

■ **Use your ears.** Remember, communication is not two monologues. If you are talking to someone, listen as well.

■ **Take your time.** Pause, ask questions, negotiate, sell, respect the other person's point of view.

■ **Get in tune.** Good communicators are very flexible. They monitor the other person's reactions and vary their delivery according to the understanding and background of the person.

■ **Be focused.** Have a reason to communicate. Don't just open your mouth. What outcome do you want from your communication? If you know what you want, you are more likely to be focused in how you communicate.

■ **Pay attention to the medium.** In business, how you communicate is often as important as what you communicate.

■ **Choose your approach.** Will your message be more effective if you speak face to face, have a meeting or write an email?

■ **Think before you speak.** People who think through what they are going to say can be a rarity in business. Many people talk in order to form thoughts; they produce a lot of noise but without much purpose.

■ **Develop your natural inquisitiveness.** Good communicators are genuinely interested in listening as well as talking. They want to gain new knowledge and hear what the other person has to say.

Take responsibility for what you say and how you say it.

1.2

Watch your facts

One of the hazards in business conversations is falling into the habit of stating 'fact' after 'fact' in an assertive manner when the statements are really just opinions. To be clear in your communication and avoid misunderstandings, learn to distinguish your facts from opinions and assertions.

When you talk, there are only a few ways in which you can say something: by asking questions, stating facts or giving opinions. If you want to communicate well in business, you need to recognize when it is appropriate to be gentle, when you should be forceful and when to be probing and challenging.

Often people state facts or offer opinions when really they should be trying to pry out information through soft questioning. So let's be clear: a fact is something that is specific enough that you can prove it with evidence.

■ **Fact.** "The economy grew by 10% year on year."
■ **Opinion.** "I am always right and you are always wrong."

The first statement is a fact and can be backed up with evidence. The second statement, on the other hand, is not a fact; it is an opinion. It is important that you don't get confused between facts and opinions, whether as a manager or an employee, or when you are selling or negotiating. If you give an opinion, it should always be made clear, usually by saying something like, "in my opinion…" or "in my way of thinking…" as a way to introduce the theme. This allows the opportunity for discussion and others to hold different views to your own.

The poorest form of communication is the overuse of assertions, as an assertion is an opinion pretending to be a fact. Because they are not prefaced by any sign that they are an opinion, the other person is encouraged to accept them as being true even if there is no hard evidence to support them.

Weak communicators use assertions in order to close down debate and discussion. They close off any room for the other person in the conversation to give their opinion. Managers who use assertions all the time soon find that they are surrounded by 'yes people' while never really finding out what is going on in their organizations.

Distinguish facts from your opinions in conversations by making it clear when it is 'just your view'.

1.3

Listen actively

Good listening skills are a vital element of good communication and help to build business relationships, whether in a team or when selling to a client. Most people think they listen, but, if you watch them closely, they are really simply working out what they are going to say as soon as they get an opportunity in the conversation.

Lots of people listen with their 'mouths' rather than their ears. They are not really listening at all. They are simply looking for a chance to speak so they can take control of the conversation – this is called selective listening.

Why is this so? They probably assume that they have more interesting, intelligent, knowledgeable or relevant things to say than the other person. Or they are mentally editing or criticizing what the other person is saying, and prejudging the outcome of the conversation.

In contrast, when you actively listen, you don't jump to conclusions about what the speaker is saying but try to see things from the other person's viewpoint. Real listening is not passive. It takes focus and energy, but the pay off is much improved communication. These are some steps you can take to listen actively:

"Silence is a source of great strength" Laozi, Chinese sage

1 **Use body language.** When you actively listen, you show the person through speech and body language that you are listening. Use eye contact and your facial expressions and gestures to show that you are listening.

2 **Be curious.** Don't pre-judge what the speaker wants to say. Be interested. What is the outcome they want? What is their motivation? What is the real reason they are talking to you?

3 **Summarize.** Repeat back what you think the speaker has just said to you. For example, "What I have heard you say is XXX." This gives the speaker the opportunity to clarify any misunderstood areas.

4 **Clarify any abstract or fuzzy terms as you go along.** This assists the speaker to recognize any gaps in the information that they are giving you. You can say, "This is what I am hearing you saying? Is this right?"

5 **Be silent when necessary.** Silence is an important part of listening. Silences in the conversation give the other person time to explore and express their thoughts fully.

Listen actively and focus on the speaker's message without prejudging the conversation.

1.4

Ask effective questions

Not enough people ask effective questions. Precise questions allow you to understand problems in a team or with your client, find out what's going on beneath the surface, defuse problem situations before they fully arise, get people to cooperate with you, find out important information, negotiate and persuade people to help and support you.

If you want to improve your communication in any business situation, then become a great questioner. You can become much more effecive in many situations by asking the right questions. This is particularly useful in challenging situations, such as if a mistake has been made or if you want to get others to agree to an idea or proposal.

Powerful questions are generally open-ended, thought-provoking or probing. This means they can't be answered with a simple yes or no answer.

'What' and 'how' questions draw out the other person and are most likely to get them to reveal their real opinions. Here are some examples you can use again and again:

"Effective questioning brings insight, which fuels curiosity, which cultivates wisdom"

Chip Bell, American writer

■ **Information-seeking questions.** These draw out additional information from the other person. "What do you mean by…?", "Tell me more about…?", "What else?"

■ **Exploratory questions.** These allow someone to think about different approaches: "Could you approach this in a different way?" "What are the possibilities here?", "What are the opportunities here?"

■ **Identifying a problem.** "What seems to be the problem?", "What is stopping you from…?", "What is your main block?", "What worries you most about…?", "How do you feel about…?"

■ **Outcome questions.** "What outcome do you want?", "If you have this, how will it effect you?", "What other factors do you need to consider?"

■ **Clarification.** "What do you mean by…?", "Could you put that another way?", "Can you give me an example?"

■ **Action.** "What will you do?", "When will you do it?", "How will I know you did it?", "What are your next steps?"

■ **Response to ideas.** "How does that sound to you?", "What benefits do you think you will gain from…?", "Does that answer the issue?"

Effective questioning combined with active listening form a fundamental set of communication skills for business.

1.5

'Chunk' appropriately

Think about the people you work with. You'll probably find that there are two types: big picture people and detail people. Big picture people like to hear little detail. Detail people don't like discussing abstract concepts. Each type will only really take in what you say to them effectively if you communicate in the right-sized 'chunk' of detail.

The simplest way to think about this is that these two different types of thinkers process information in distinct ways. This is important to know and recognize if you want to influence other people with your communication.

Once you know the difference is there, look out for signs of how much detail or abstract information a person appears to be able to process, and respond flexibly in your communication.

■ **Big picture people.** Another term for big picture people is 'global thinkers'. If you are communicating information to a global thinker, stop giving lots of detailed information and focus on the big picture. If you focus too much on detail, they will rapidly become bored or overwhelmed, and fail to either understand what you are saying or be

one minute wonder Your flexibility in communication will make an enormous difference to your effectiveness. Do you know what level of detail you like to communicate most? If you know your habits, you can challenge yourself to become a more flexible communicator.

influenced by you. The best thing to say to a global thinker is: "Here's the big picture…". Stay abstract and don't give too many details. If you need to give detailed information, then give the big picture first: "Here's the big picture… now I am going to give you some details."

■ **Detail people.** Detail people, on the other hand, need to start with detail before they can become engaged with what you have to say about the wider idea. They can't handle it if you start talking too conceptually. Say to them, "Here are the details." Be specific and don't use abstractions. If you need them to focus on the detail and keep an eye on the big picture, give them both in this way: "Here are the details… and here's the big picture."

Find out which members of your team and which of your clients like to communicate predominately in which way, and you will gain much more control over your communication.

Work out whether your team are big picture or detail communicators.

1.6

Choose your words

There is another key difference between people that's worth paying attention to. It is what's sometimes called the preferred language type. In everyday language, we often use words associated with the senses: seeing, hearing and feeling. This relates to how we process information. If you communicate according to the preferred choice of the listener, they will be more open to what you say.

People who use a lot of words associated with seeing understand better if you use similar words back to them, and it's the same for other senses, such as hearing and feeling.

■ **Visual.** Here are some examples of the kinds of phrases you can use when communicating with a visually inclined person: "Appears to me", "Get a perspective on", "In view of", "Eye to eye", "Hazy idea", "Dim view", "In light of", "Mental image", "Paint a picture", "Looks like", "Short sighted", "Pretty as a picture".

■ **Auditory.** Other people use words associated with hearing and sound. Use these types of phrases to make them feel 'in tune': "Clearly expressed", "Earful", "Loud and clear", "Tongue-tied", "Power

> **"The most basic of all human needs is the need to understand and be understood. The best way to understand people is to listen to them"**
>
> **Ralph Nichols, business coach**

of speech", "Rings a bell", "Clear as a bell", "To tell the truth", "Outspoken", "Tuned in/out", "Voiced an opinion".

■ **Kinaesthetic.** Finally, some people prefer words associated with feeling, known as the kinaesthetic sense: "Come to grips with", "Firm foundations", "Cool, calm and collected", "Get a handle on", "Get the drift of", "Get in touch with", "Grapple with", "Fight your corner".

It may take you a while to get to grips with this concept, but if you tune in to the different ways in which different people speak, you will begin to notice that they use varying amounts of sense-specific words. Once you have become attuned to how other people speak, you can adapt your own language accordingly. This will build your ability to be a highly flexible communicator. You can also practise by reading. Notice how different writers are more visual, auditory or kinaesthetic in the way that they write.

The sense someone chooses corresponds to how they process thoughts so this is a very vital piece of communication to observe.

Pick your words carefully according to who you are communicating with.

Body basics

In conversation people tend to pay attention only to the words they use. However, communication takes place on many levels, some conscious, others unconscious. By understanding your own body language, you will create a stronger business presence and make a favourable impression every time you meet a colleague or client. Reading other people's body language will help you become aware of subtle dynamics and deeper levels of communication.

2.1

Stand out at first glance

"Trust me", says the salesperson you meet for the first time. But something about them looks shifty. How long will it take you to get over that first impression? Our first impressions are formed within as little as 10 seconds, and the first impression is hard to shift, so you need to make sure you've made a positive one.

It's not only your words that make an impression when you meet someone but also your body language. Whether you are talking to someone over the phone, introducing yourself face to face or simply walking into a room and looking around without speaking, your body is saying even more than what's coming out of your mouth.

one minute wonder Practise putting authority into what you say. Say something serious in a squeaky voice and you will notice not only how the words are undermined but also how you have to change your breathing to do this. Now deepen your breathing and notice how your voice gains power.

Psychology Professor Albert Mehrabian produced the now most used model of communication in the 1970s. He showed that:

■ **55% of communication** is down to the way you stand or sit, your gestures and facial expressions. Some of this body language is very obvious, while other signals will only be picked up unconsciously.
■ **7–10% of communication** comes from the actual words you use.
■ **35–38% of communication** is how you say things: how loudly you speak, your accent and how deep or high is your tone of voice.

Of course, if you are on a telephone, you have only your voice to work with, but still watch how you are standing or sitting and how you are breathing, as they will all affect how your voice sounds.

So, what was going on with that shifty, untrustworthy person you met for the first time? Well, he or she was probably saying the right things but thinking something different. That showed up in, or leaked into, their body language.

Pay attention to what you say but also make sure that you believe what you say. If you don't, your audience will pick up immediately that something is not quite right. They won't necessarily know what is not right, but instinctively they will know that they don't feel comfortable with you, and that isn't a positive in business.

Watch what you are saying with your body; it's an even more important communicator than your words.

2.2

Be aware of personal space

Have you ever had to move away from a colleague or client because you felt as if they were intruding into your personal space? It is such an uncomfortable feeling, and, if the person continues to crowd us, we will feel very unfriendly towards them and will be unlikely to want to do business with them.

Our personal space is composed of several invisible zones around us. If someone intrudes into these, we begin to feel very uncomfortable. We will let a lover or a close family member come very close to us, but a stranger or a work colleague cannot come as close.

The closest invisible zone (from the skin to 18 inches/45 cm around us) is called the personal zone and is reserved for people we are happy to be touched by or to touch. If a stranger comes into this intimate space, it will feel as if a warning bell has immediately gone off. You will sense the intrusion and want to move away. Around 30% of people will move within one minute of someone invading their space.

The need for personal space varies from culture to culture, so it is something that is very important to become aware of, especially if you are doing business internationally.

"The emotional brain responds to an event more quickly than the thinking brain"

Daniel Goleman, American author

There are even differences between people from the town and from the country in terms of how much space they need around them. This means becoming aware of not only people coming into your space but also how you might be unconsciously becoming a 'space invader' as well.

To avoid becoming a 'space invader', follow these simple rules:

1 Pay attention to the body language of the other people you meet in any business situation, particularly when abroad. Judge the distance people commonly stand apart.

2 If someone starts moving back from you while in conversation, don't pursue them, but allow them to keep some distance between the two of you.

3 If they become comfortable in your company, they will close the gap a little or you will at least see their body language relax. You will probably feel the difference too, as the atmosphere warms and you feel more in rapport.

Be conscious of the invisible zones of personal space and avoid being a 'space invader'.

2.3

Practise your handshake

Why are handshakes so important in business? Handshakes are one of the few times we let a stranger come into close contact with us and come into our invisble personal zone. Touching someone is such a personal interaction that, when someone touches us, we form an immediate impression of them.

A handshake is such a simple thing on the surface. After all, what are you doing? Just extending your right hand and shaking the other person's right hand. But there are so many variations, partly due to personal preference but also to cultural acceptability.

A firm handshake gives a totally different impression to a light handshake. Too firm, and you come across as if you are trying to control the other person. But too soft, and it becomes the dreaded 'wet fish' handshake – a limp hand that lacks all authority and is very uncomfortable for the other person.

Here are a few pointers to the perfect handshake, which will make you appear businesslike and competent.

one minute wonder Anxiety shows in the hands. It makes them feel cool or clammy, which is very unpleasant for the person shaking those hands. Conversely, warm hands make us assume that the person is warm and trustworthy. So, smile and be relaxed when you shake hands, and the other person will feel it in your handshake.

■ **Watch your grip.** Ideally it should be strong and steady rather than held lightly with the fingertips just touching the other person's hand. The fingertip grip can give the impression of a lack of confidence. In the perfect business handshake, your hands will be level with the other person's. Your grip will be firm but neither too tight nor too loose. It will feel open and self-confident, whether you are a man or a woman.

■ **Keep it simple.** Some people will pat you on the shoulder or touch you on the elbow or wrist while they shake your hand. Others may place their hand on top of, rather than level with, yours. Be careful of any of these gestures and affectations, as they may be perceived as either too intimate or too dominant.

■ **Don't hurry.** Hold the other person's hand firmly and pump it three times or so. Only one pump, and you will come across as tentative. Give them time and attention when you greet them, and you will make a far better first impression.

■ **Learn any local variants.** The handshake is recognized in most cultures. However if you are doing business abroad then it is worth checking to see if any variants or alternatives are more common in business, for example bowing or praying-style gestures in parts of Asia.

Practise having a firm, level handshake where you take the other person's hand and pump three times.

2.4

Use eye contact carefully

What happens when you look at someone and they break away and won't look at you directly? You probably become a little suspicious about them. Direct eye contact, in contrast, can be seen as more open. Make sure you use appropriate eye contact, even if it doesn't come naturally to you.

The key to eye contact is to be aware of who you are talking to. When you look directly into someone's eyes, it is regarded positively in Western business practice, for there the eyes are very much regarded as 'windows to the soul'. Direct eye contact is equated with being honest and trustworthy. Indeed, eye contact is so powerful in the West that

case study A trip to the zoo can be surprisingly instructive for learning about eye contact. An ape that stares directly at another ape, for example, is showing that they are the dominant animal. Humans are no different. If you were to stare directly at someone and hold your gaze, the other person would begin to feel

the phrase 'wouldn't look you in the eye' is used in English to imply that someone might be shifty. This isn't the case in all cultures though, and even in the West, prolonged eye contact can be disconcerting.

In a naturally flowing conversation, we tend to look at the other person more when we are listening than when we are talking. However, men and women with particular status, power or expertise within business tend to look more when they are speaking. Women need to be particularly conscious of eye contact. Research shows that, outside a business setting, a woman will generally look at a man when they are not being looked at, but will look away when the man looks directly at them. This is interpreted as submissive in many cultures.

Key points for using eye contact to appear confident:

■ **Adopt a business persona.** If lowering your eyes modestly is a natural habit for you, when you come to business you may find that you are giving out signals that you are submissive or in a lower position than you really are. Scrutinize and become aware of your habits, and, if necessary, learn to 'perform' differently in the business environment.

■ **Look while you are talking.** If you want to have more control in a presentation setting, adopt the habit of looking directly at your audience when you are talking. It signals an air of strength and confidence.

Use direct eye contact, but beware of appearing too dominant.

as if you were trying to control them. It would either force them into a battle with you, in which they would try to 'stare you out', or they will break eye contact and glance away in a submissive gesture. These subtle forms of eye contact communication at the zoo are mirrored every day in the business world.

2.5

Show you're friendly

Every time you talk to someone, your body language either says, 'Welcome, I am open to meet you and talk to you', or 'I am closed. I don't want to listen to you. Go away.' Even without speaking, we give out these welcoming or off-putting signals. What you feel shows up clearly in your posture, gestures and facial expressions.

Signs of positive, open lines of communication

■ **Open stance.** Uncrossing your legs and arms and directly facing the other person shows that you are eager to talk or listen to them. Combine this with good eye contact for great open communication skills.

■ **Friendly expression.** Generally, when your body language is open, you don't have any defenses up because you have decided that you are with a 'friend'. Your shoulders will be relaxed and you might be smiling or certainly have a relaxed expression on your face.

■ **Leaning forward.** If someone has open body language and is leaning forward to catch what is said, they are interested and accepting what you are saying. If you are selling, this is a great time to close a deal.

one minute wonder Stay 'open for business' as much as possible on a day-to-day basis by keeping your attitude genuinely engaged. Our attitudes are contagious, so, if you are happy, interested and relaxed, you will have welcoming body language, and this will 'infect' the people around you.

■ **Response and interaction.** When someone sees you, they will 'read' from your body alone that you are pleased to meet them or eager to learn something new. This is what you are aiming for; it's what can help you do good business, whether in negotiations, clinching sales or motivating a team of workers.

Signs of disengagement from communication

Boredom, dislike and defensiveness all show up in closed body language. If you are talking to a group of people and being boring, you will see your audience switching off through body language signals.

■ **Crossed arms and legs.** These are giveaways that things are not going well. It's a clear sign of unresponsiveness. Avoiding eye contact is another sign that someone may feel uncomfortable with you or not be interested in what you have to say.

■ **Leaning back.** If someone is leaning back but looking relaxed, they may be listening passively, in which case you need to either give them the space to think or perhaps engage them more actively. If they have closed body language and are fiddling or have their feet pointing towards the door, they have given up and have their minds elsewhere. You'll need to act quickly to draw their interest back.

Know your open and closed body language signals.

2.6

Be authoritative

Being able to use power and authority appropriately can be very important in business. For example, you will want to look authoritative when you present to a client or to colleagues. Body language plays a key part in how much authority you convey.

Firstly, relax. Relaxed shoulders and facial expressions show that you are confident and in charge of your emotions. They say, 'I am not threatened by anything or anybody'. Relax and, even if you aren't confident to begin with, you will start to feel more confident and people will respond in kind.

Next, pay attention to the four 'S's:

■ **Stance** is very authoritative. Powerful people stand and sit solidly, with a straight back. This gives them a look of youth and energy.

> **case study** I had a work colleague called called Wenda, who, although very capable in her job, couldn't avoid making gestures that were perceived as submissive. Tall and slightly shy, she would automatically lower her head when in conversation, even with workers of

■ **Size** matters too. Unconsciously, height and size equal authority. If you want to look more powerful and you are short and slim, you need to draw on your posture and artificial aids. Stand tall or use high heels. It really will make a difference. Keep an erect posture with your head held high. You can create relative height by standing while someone else is sitting. The proof of how much this matters can be seen in US presidential elections, where the rule of thumb is that the tallest candidate wins the election. This is because we unconsciously equate height with importance: big things matter more than small things.

■ **Space** is the third S. A powerful person stakes out more territory than a less powerful one. He may create more space by drawing his chair back from the table or even by just putting his hands on his hips while standing, as if to say this extra little bit of space belongs to me.

■ **Straddles** is the fourth S. In a standing straddle you have your legs wide apart, taking up space and showing that you will 'stand your ground'. In a seated straddle, you sit with your legs apart, across the chair and facing the back of the chair.

Keep an erect, relaxed stance and you will immediately start to radiate a positive air of authority.

equal or lower status. It meant that she lacked authority and wasn't regarded as highly as she might have been. The way she overcame this obstacle to her progress was to actively practise looking tall and powerful until eventually it became quite natural to her.

2.7

Be culturally appropriate

It is highly likely that in this global business world you will do business with colleagues and clients from other cultures, even if you don't travel for your job. Do you expect other cultures to adapt to your way of doing things? You will be more effective if you are flexible enough to adopt other people's ways as well.

We use gestures to give instructions, such as pointing out a direction, but also to threaten. In business, we might use a gesture to illustrate the message we are making in conversation or in a business presentation. Gestures vary enormously from one culture to another. While the basics of some body language is similar, all over the world people use their hands and bodies to communicate different messages. Here are some examples of gestures that vary from culture to culture:

■ **Beckoning.** In Asian countries beckoning is done with the palm facing down. Avoid pointing with the fingers. In Western countries, the palm faces upwards.

■ **Smiling.** This doesn't always equate with happiness. It may be covering embarrassed, angry, sad, apologetic or guilty feelings.

■ **Open mouths.** It can be considered rude not to cover your mouth when you are yawning in some cultures. In others, laughing without putting your hand in front of your mouth is frowned upon.

■ **Leg crossing.** If you are travelling on business, watch what your host does. Crossing your legs at the ankles may be more appropriate than having the legs crossed at the knees.

■ **Touch.** It has become more acceptable to kiss or touch the arm when greeting close colleagues in the West. However, touch and body contact is definitely not acceptable in many other cultures.

The key in the global village is to be aware. Look out for gestures you don't recognize. If in doubt of the meaning, don't ignore or mimic them. Always ask questions first.

Gestures can mean very different things across cultures; if in doubt, check the meaning first.

Team talk

Whatever business you are in, it's highly likely you'll need to work in a team at some point. Communication inside a team can act as a key motivator or de-motivator. Good communication can cause a team to bond and grow stronger; poor communication leads to a lack of trust, misunderstandings and conflict. In this chapter you will discover some of the secrets behind effective team talk: how to positively impact your team and your organization as a whole.

3.1

Be aware of dynamics

In every team there are certain team dynamics. There'll be people who like each other and others who don't get on, as well as the group's leaders and followers. Be aware of the dynamics if you want to form a happy team or influence your colleagues.

Many of the dynamics in a team are unconscious. Regardless of the titles and status an organization has bestowed on you and your work colleagues, the real pecking order is decided by power.

So who are the leaders and followers in your organization? In your smaller team? Are there power struggles? What about you? How much power or influence do you have?

one minute wonder When you spot someone using power plays by showing dominant body language, be careful about challenging their territory. You are likely to get a negative backlash. Always get into rapport first and win them over so that they'll let you into their territory and relax.

Body language lets you know what's really going on. Once you know the unconscious hierarchy, then you know who's important. Here are some of the secret clusters of movements you may notice to let you know who is the real boss in your team:

■ **Relaxed manner.** Dominant people are relaxed because they are in charge. Watch out for your colleague who has his feet up on the desk while he is talking to you. He thinks he owns this territory.

■ **Casual approach.** The same goes if he is leaning back in his chair against a wall or a desk with his hands clasped behind his head.

■ **Chair straddling.** This stance, straddling a chair back to front, is a real giveaway. It shows that he owns the space around the chair and is asserting his power (see Secret 2.6).

Now, who likes each other in your team?

■ **Copying.** Watch to see if colleagues are copying your gestures and posture. If they do you are in rapport with them.

■ **Intimacy.** People who like each other have good eye contact, smile a lot and tend to face directly towards each other while talking. They are likely to stand or sit close to the people they like.

If a member of the team is not in rapport, with poor eye contact and a tendency to turn away from the others, they are not in agreement with the group or do not feel close to them.

Watch out for dominant body language signals from colleagues to find out who's got the power.

3.2

Take people into your confidence

Pretty much everyone loves knowing something they think others don't know. When you share a secret with someone, it makes them feel close to you. That creates a lot of trust between you and your listener. They feel that you must trust them if you are willing to share something so important and intimate.

Sharing secrets is a great thing to do if you want to create a feeling of intimacy, and it works as well in business as in personal life. You create a feeling of trust between the two of you but, more than that, you start to get the same behaviour back in return.

one minute wonder Here's how to get started: "Off the record, I just want to tell you about…", "No one knows this but I want to tell you before anyone else…", "I shouldn't be telling anyone about this because it hasn't been publicized yet…", "Can you promise you won't tell anyone yet but…".

"Secrets are things we give to others to keep for us"

Elbert Hubbard, 19th century American writer and publisher

The benefits of sharing secrets to develop better lines of communication in a business framework are simple:

■ **If you confide in people, they are more likely to confide in you.** It leads to more open communication and a feeling of 'team'. This is because team members start to take off the 'masks' that all of us to some extent wear as a defence in a business situation.

■ **Sharing secrets lets you get to know people better.** It is also a great tool for influencing and persuading others. The more you know about what other people want and need, the more you can help them get what they want. So, as well as sharing secrets with colleagues, you can create a feeling of intimacy between yourself and your clients in the same way. It's the basic law of friendship. If you think a person has your best interests at heart and they then ask you to do something, you are much more likely to want to respond to that request.

Of course, I am not saying that you should tell everyone your deepest and darkest personal secrets, or indeed anything that is unethical for you to talk about in a business situation, but do communicate the feeling that you are letting them know a piece of exclusive news ahead of anyone else.

Share confidences to create trust in your team and strengthen the bonds of communication between its members.

3.3

Show gratitude

"Thank you" is such a simple thing to say, but how often do you, as a boss or as a colleague, remember to express appreciation? The norm in many organizations is to criticize and find fault, but often managers and colleagues don't stop to give the time to say what is working well in a team.

It doesn't matter what your position is in the team. Whether you are the person in charge or the one with the lowest status in the team, you can improve communication throughout the team by showing when you are happy with someone for something they have done for you. Every time you focus on others rather than yourself and say what is right about what they have achieved, you help to build a positive team spirit.

Research in schools shows that teachers who praise their students for the positive actions while showing them how to stretch themselves in their goals have a very empowering effect on those around them. Students feel that they have a firm foundation of support and so feel more able to grow and develop and, if necessary, take calculated risks.

> **"** A good team is a great place to be, exciting, stimulating, supportive, successful. A bad team is horrible, a sort of human prison **"**

Charles Handy, business author

When we leave school, we no longer have teachers who are paid to help us learn and develop. In a good business, the manager will coach and mentor others. If that is not part of the culture of your organization, however, it is something you can start to change through your own actions, whatever position you are in.

■ **Appreciation.** Say "thank you" to show that you are supportive and approving of what others are trying to accomplish within the team.

■ **Attentiveness.** Take the time to listen and give attention to the people around you. It is extraordinary how such a very simple action can not only make you skilled at communication but also put you way ahead of the majority of people in business in interaction with others.

■ **Congratulation.** Offer praise when a colleague or one of your team has performed either well on a specific task or consistently in their work over time. It maximizes the positive feeling surrounding successful business, and also encourages your colleagues to maintain their high levels or consistency, which might otherwise dip.

Show support to your team through listening and attention, and let them know when they are doing well.

3.4

Establish a rapport

Creating a rapport with people ensures that you build strong working relationships based on a mutual feeling of trust and respect. When we are in rapport we feel that we like, and are like, the other person. Rapport works as a bridge between people from any walk of life and it is built through powerful communication skills.

Have you ever met someone for the first time and felt a sense of connection and harmony with them? But, on other occasions, you meet people who don't seem engaged, or trustworthy or warm. The difference is rapport – that sense of being on the same unconscious and conscious wavelength that makes you feel really comfortable with the other person.

one minute wonder You can create rapport just by matching tones of voice and the words a person uses. But be cautious. Don't mimic accents or you may be hounded out of your business meeting. If in doubt, just keep it simple by using some key jargon that the other person uses.

"Never be haughty to the humble; never be humble to the haughty"

Jefferson Davis, American president 1861–5

Sometimes it happens automatically but you can also create rapport deliberately by using this simple method. Think about people you get on with easily. Without noticing, you probably use similar ways of talking, words and body language. Next time you walk into a meeting with a group of people present, notice that the people who are feeling close to each other are sitting or standing in similar positions, using similar or the same gestures. This is called matching or mirroring.

■ **Matching.** This is where one person uses the same communication as the other person – their tone of voice, certain words and phrases, their breathing rate and their body language. If one person crosses their arms, the other person does the same. One person uses a particular phrase and the other picks up the same words.

■ **Mirroring.** With mirroring, one person is the mirror image of the other. If one person crosses their right leg over their left, the other crosses their left leg over their right.

If you use these techniques deliberately, you can create exactly the same feeling of rapport as if it happened instinctively. Observe the person's body language. Watch for gestures and look at posture, but be subtle. Avoid obvious mimicry. Matching and mirroring should occur outside the other person's conscious awareness, otherwise people will think you are trying to mock them.

Match and mirror to create a happy, trusting feeling.

3.5

Give good feedback

Giving good feedback is important if you are managing a team, or coaching or training individuals. Feedback is a key communication tool which allows people to learn from their mistakes and successes. It is important, though, that when you give feedback, you do it in a way that it will be heard constructively.

There is a difference between criticizing someone and giving feedback. Good feedback allows the listener to learn from their mistakes or weak areas and to change. Criticism, on the other hand, is often just a way to belittle or put blame on another person.

Good feedback should be brief and concise, and couched positively. It should also be owned by you: "I find that…" rather than "you are…".

one minute wonder When giving feedback, use positive phrases. Say "do this" rather than "don't do that". The brain hears the positive wording and reacts by forming a picture of the new goal which helps clarify the action needed to achieve it.

There are different ways of giving feedback to someone. One of the easiest is the **sandwich** structure:

1 First say what was good about a person's performance: this is the top slice of bread in your sandwich.

2 Next say what would make it even better next time (three areas for development, for example): this is the filling.

3 Finally, finish on a positive note. Say overall what was good about the person's performance.

The **BOOST** feedback model offers a more complex approach.

■ **B = Balanced.** Get the person to think about both their areas of strength and where development is needed.

■ **O = Observed.** Communicate what you have observed about the other person's behaviour.

■ **O = Objective.** Avoid being subjective, prejudiced or judgmental about the other person. Make sure your feedback is only about what the person is doing or has done, not about who they are.

■ **S = Specific.** For each piece of feedback about behaviour, give one or two specific examples that you have observed. Generalized feedback is not easy for the listener to learn from, so, instead of saying, "you are sloppy…", it would be better to say, "when you do XXX…".

■ **T = Timely.** Any feedback you give is best given as soon as possible after the behaviour you have observed. Timely advice allows the listener to reflect on what they have done immediately.

Give constructive feedback using the sandwich or BOOST models.

3.6

Be persuasive

It doesn't matter what your position is in a team or in the overall organization, good persuaders are very valued. To be a persuasive communicator, the key thing is to understand two different types of people: 'towards' people and 'away from' people. Both want something. Can you supply it?

'Towards' people are motivated by what they want to have, be or do. For example, "I want to have a salary rise", "I want to be successful in this project", "I want to do this by the end of today".

If you want to motivate these people, you need to communicate with them by using language that offers them more of what they want to have, be or do. Suppose, for example, you want to persuade a colleague to help you to write a report. You need to find out what they are motivated by.

■ **What are their goals?** What do they want more of? Do they want to have more, do more or be more?
■ **What can you offer them?** Whatever it is they want, if you offer it to them, you will persuade them to help you.

one minute wonder To be really persuasive, paint a vivid picture of the future resulting from acceptance of your proposal. Get the other person to imagine what it will be like now, i.e. the benefits they will have when they accept your proposal.

Here's an example for an approach when dealing with a **'towards'** person: "By helping me write this report, you will be noticed by the important people in the company. Ultimately it may help you get a promotion or a salary rise."

'Away from' people are motivated by what they want to avoid having, doing or being. For example, "I don't want to have no money", "I don't want to take on more work", "I don't want to be more stressed".

To motivate 'away from' people, communicate with them in their terms. Offer them less of what they want to avoid having, doing or being. Suppose, for example, you again want to get your colleague to help you write a report.

■ **What are their avoidance goals?** In other words, what do they want to avoid having, doing and being?
■ **What can you offer them?** Offer them the chance to have less of what they want to avoid by helping you.

Here's an example if you're dealing with an 'away from' person: "By helping me write this report, you will free me up to help you with the project that is stressing you, so you can avoid being stressed this week."

Notice which of your colleagues are 'away from' and which are 'towards' people. It's the key to their motivation.

3.7

Be a coach

Use communication as a learning tool. A team that continually challenges itself to grow is going to be a very effective team and contribute well to an organization. Communication and learning are interlinked, of course, and here are some of the key factors and techniques that will help you coach yourself or others to keep learning every day.

■ **Ask questions.** If you don't know something or are unclear, always ask questions. It's the most effective way to develop as an employee.
■ **Suggest ideas.** Don't keep quiet and just go along with others. Speak up and give voice to your ideas.

case study Anita was put in charge of a team that had had problems with the previous boss. She soon discovered that the team had stagnated and no-one was progressing in their career. She came up with this simple and effective guidance. "If there is a problem in the team, don't dwell on it or on the past. Focus instead on what future opportunities there may be.

■ Admit mistakes and weaknesses. Convert your mistakes into learning. Remember there's no failure, only feedback. Use everything you do as an opportunity to learn.

■ Reflect and review. Say what has worked and what hasn't, either to yourself or out loud to your boss or a coach. Learn every day.

■ Discuss what you have learnt. It will stop you from repeating the same mistakes or rushing around just being active for the sake of it.

■ Don't rubbish other people's ideas. You can always learn from what other people come up with. Probe and find out more instead.

■ Don't blame other people. When things go wrong, blaming others will just stop you learning. You will be the person who suffers.

■ Don't tell people only what they want to hear. If there is bad news, tell it straight and use your rapport skills.

■ Be observant. Notice when people are comfortable and uncomfortable with your communication. This will let you know when to offer support and when to hold back.

■ Be encouraging and supportive. In your communication with others when they are carrying out a task, use the BOOST model when you give feedback. This will help you to create trust.

Be honest and learn through your communication in order to become a great coach for everyone.

This will encourage our creativity and get us all to think about improvements and motivation." She asked the team to agree to the new way of thinking. After three months she found that communication had improved considerably, the team had become much more productive and members started asking her for development opportunities within the organization.

Making the most of meetings

Meetings are opportunities for you to be recognized inside an organization, to get your message across with authority and, if necessary, to get consensus or approval to take action. If you want to get rave reviews for your meeting style, you need to learn some tricks and tools for influencing others so that everybody leaves the meeting remembering what you said. Pay attention to these meeting secrets and the business will start to pay attention to you.

4.1

Plan and prepare

Any business discussion should be tackled in a businesslike way. You probably wouldn't launch a new product into a market without knowing quite a lot about the market, your product and what you intend to get out of the launch. I am sure you would do your research on your competition as well. So schedule time to plan and prepare.

As soon as you think of scheduling a meeting, stop and ask yourself: do you really need to have a meeting face-to-face? Could you say this by phone or on an email?

Businesses waste hundreds of hours every year on unnecessary meetings. However, if you do think you need to sit down and speak to someone, think about what you want to get out of the meeting. This doesn't mean some vague goal such as it will get people talking or maybe you should let people know that this is going on in the company. It needs to be specific:

■ "What do I want to happen in the short term as a result of communicating this? What about the long term?"

Take some time to think about what your criteria will be for judging the success of the meeting.

■ "How will I know when I have achieved this? What is my evidence going to be that I have been successful?"

You may find with a clear goal in mind that everything will run smoothly or you may need to be flexible in the way you communicate. It's worth thinking ahead about who will be present in the meeting.

■ "What are they likely to want, and what obstacles might I run into during the meeting?"

By asking yourself "what happens if X occurs?" you can think about your options for communicating in different ways. Once you've been through the process of considering these questions, go ahead and develop your agenda. As you do so, bear in mind that everybody invited to the meeting ideally should have enough information to be able to make a decision on about two thirds of the points on the agenda.

Then, with the right people invited to your meeting, it's time to put your message across.

Be clear about your intended outcome for the meeting and the obstacles that are likely to stand in your way.

4.2

Pay attention to your audience

Strong communicators are flexible communicators. They don't just use stock speeches that they give under all circumstances. They vary their messages to suit the audience in front of them. Of course, you still need to prepare what you are going to say in advance, but at the same time be ready to make changes according to the situation.

You may be very good at presenting formally standing up in front of a small group, or talking at a large meeting. Alternatively, you may excel in informal meetings. Ideally, though, you want to become a flexible, confident speaker whatever the situation – big, small, formal, informal, within the organization or to outside clients.

By keeping your attention on the needs of your audience, you can become a confident communicator in all these circumstances. Here are a few guidelines to build your speaking skills.

■ **Choose your words.** One of the first things to think about is whether everybody in the meeting is a native speaker of your language. If not, you may need to simplify what you say.

one minute wonder One easy way to give simple information without seeming patronizing is to use phrases such "as of course you know..." or "obviously in this kind of situation one of the answers would be...". It helps maintain a rapport as well.

■ **Avoid jargon.** Next, think about how much the audience already knows about your subject. Be careful about using abbreviations and jargon that may be unfamiliar.

■ **Find the right level.** Be careful not to patronize. Keep things simple, but, if you are not sure if it is too simple, check with your audience: "Is this the right level of detail?"

■ **Use additional methods sparingly.** It's okay to use Powerpoint, flipcharts and handouts to emphasize the points you want to make, but this can make things very formal, so pay attention to your audience.

■ **Don't become distracted.** If you use props, still watch your audience, not the props. If you lose focus on your audience, they will lose interest in what you have to say.

■ **Maintain concentration on your audience.** If you use Power-point, do check you have the right slides in front of you. One brief glance is enough, though. Then make your point to the audience.

If you are not sure how you come across in different situations, ask a colleague or friend to video you presenting or talking to them. You can learn a lot by watching your gestures, and posture and how you talk – even to one other person.

Use props, but make sure that they help rather than hinder your message.

4.3

Stand (or sit) tall

Good posture has an amazing effect on the people watching you. It doesn't matter whether you are standing or sitting, you can maintain an erect, strong posture. This will greatly reinforce whatever message you want to get across.

Many office workers develop very poor posture habits. Sitting at computers day after day, carrying big bags and feeling stressed all contribute to poor posture. This means that we don't stand up straight but tend to hunch our backs and often breathe in a shallow manner. This carries through to the voice, making it sound thin and strained.

It is un-relaxing for any audience to listen to a stressed-sounding voice. If one person in a group is breathing shallowly, the other people tend to empathetically do the same. They pick up your anxiety and

case study A few years back, I noticed a transformation in a colleague called Ros. After sustaining a back injury while gardening, she embarked on a programme of rehabilitation that involved regular exercise and a specific focus on improving her posture. As her body's strength and flexibility increased, so too did her ability

start to feel the same way themselves. This makes a very unpleasant experience for the whole group.

Standing or sitting with shoulders forward and a hunch in your back is obviously bad for the health of your body. However, what this kind of posture also does is send a visual signal to your audience that you lack authority. Powerful body language is centred and erect.

1 Change your posture by straightening your spine and relaxing your shoulders. Let your head rest comfortably and evenly on your shoulders, neither forward nor back.

2 Check that you are balanced equally between the right and left sides of your body.

3 Take big, deep breaths and notice that immediately you begin to feel more comfortable inside yourself.

Change your posture and you will transform the way you come across, and what you are saying will be received warmly and with attention by your audience.

Use your breathing to relax and centre your body to make yourself a more powerful presenter.

to communicate more powerfully and effectively. What was most notable was how the perception of her changed within the organization. People listened to her more intently, sought her help and opinions more frequently and she became a more respected member of the company.

4.4

Keep the discussion relevant

As all employees know, if there is time to fill it gets filled, efficiently or not. Whether you set aside one hour for a meeting or two hours, it will probably take the alloted amount of time or longer. If you don't want to just fill up time with useless chatter, you need to pay constant attention to keeping the focus relevant to the issues under discussion.

If you are clear about what you want to communicate during the meeting and what point you want to reach by the end, you should find it easy to keep things on track. But this will only happen if you tell everyone right at the beginning of the meeting what it is you are wanting to achieve.

Next, get people on board with what you want to achieve. Use your rapport skills to win them over. As soon as you have come up with an outcome for the meeting, ask them to agree to what you want to achieve. If you maintain a sense of rapport with other people, they are going to be much more open to persuasion.

Here's a really useful question you can ask all the way throughout the meeting to see if your discussions are on track.

■ "How does (this point or discussion) relate to the outcome we have agreed on for this meeting?"

This question is easy to remember and use and makes sure that anything that is said is relevant to the central aim of the meeting. It's said that any time someone goes off on a detour in a meeting, the discussion takes at least 20 minutes to get back to the main subject. So it's really worth using a simple strategy such as this to maintain direction.

You can also agree with your colleagues that anyone present can use this to challenge anybody who seems to be going off track. Once you agree this, whoever is talking has to be prepared to justify how the point they're making fits with the aim of the meeting.

If, after having asked the question, you all agree that the person speaking has moved away from the main point of the meeting, you can say, "I would like to ask you to backtrack", and then simply return to the last relevant point.

Key points:
■ Set out your aims for the meeting.
■ Get everyone to agree to the aims.
■ Keep the discussion relevant to achieving those aims.

Make sure you bring the meeting back all the time to the central outcome you have thought through in advance.

4.5

Be a story teller

Imagine that you are walking along a narrow road. You have been walking for five miles and are running out of steam. Along comes a car and offers you a ride. That's what is happening to our company right now. We are losing energy and we need a bigger company to give us some money to keep us going.

Information and facts are interesting up to a point, but they simply aren't memorable and don't grab the attention in the way that stories and metaphors do. That's why it's important to be a story teller, and use analogies such as the one above to illustrate ideas.

It is human nature to love stories and metaphors because we relate to them much more than facts. This is because the brain thinks with images. Feed it with pictures, such as a tired walker being offered a lift in a car, and you will be able to make your point far more easily and convincingly than if you just say something like: We are running out of money and we need financial help to keep going. A metaphor is simply more memorable.

We use metaphors naturally in speech all the time in English: that idea will sink like a stone, it's a long, winding path ahead, that's sticking out like a sore thumb, this economic storm is going through consumer confidence like a hurricane. Here are some pointers to the benefits of using them in business situations.

■ **To fire the imagination.** Effective metaphors can be short or long; the best really capture the imagination and make the listener relate them to their situation without needing further explanation from the speaker.
■ **To bring freshness to ideas.** By using an analogy, you can make people look at a situation in a fresh way or from a new angle.
■ **To be really persuasive.** They work at an unconscious level, so the listener takes exactly what they need to from the story or idea.

Using metaphors is an excellent way to introduce new ideas and to overcome potential resistance to them. It is far more effective than using facts and logic alone.

Stories spark the imagination and keep your audience engaged.

4.6

Keep it short and sweet

Meetings drift when people start filling up 'air time' for the sake of it. The most effective communicators don't do this. They know what they want to communicate, and when they have done so they shut up. If you haven't learnt this lesson you'll be talking too often and for too long, and that'll be why people are looking out of the window when you speak!

When conversing in a meeting, choose your moment to speak carefully. When you do speak, keep it simple and to the point. There is never a need in a meeting to speak for too long.

In fact, the longer someone talks the less and less effective the communication generally becomes as they go on. You can probably think of occasions when someone who is presenting to you talked for too long. What happened? You probably stopped listening and stopped learning. Parents often get this wrong: if they go on and on when rebuking a child, the child ceases to listen at all.

Sometimes in a meeting it is far more authoritative to make a shorter point. So cut the waffle and keep it short and sweet by following these essential four rules:

one minute wonder If you keep doing what you've always done, you'll keep getting what you've always got. Next time you are in a meeting and sense resistance, keep quiet. To what or whom have you not paid attention? Listen and learn.

1 **Know your outcome.** Know what you want to achieve. If you don't have a reason to speak, well, just don't speak.

2 **Listen.** If you just speak for the sake of it, you will not connect to other people through what you say. You are also less likely to listen properly.

3 **Learn.** Other people have views about what you have said. If you stop talking and listen, you will learn and maybe achieve your outcome more quickly.

4 **Leave space.** Give other people the space to respond to what you say and you will weed out any objections early on as well as finding out about different perspectives.

By speaking too long, we bore our listeners. As a result, the next time you come to speak in a meeting your listeners will be prepared – but, unfortunately, to not bother paying attention. If you really drone on and on, they may even start not turning up at all after a while.

If you start noticing resistance to your ideas in meetings, reconsider your approach. It may not be that you haven't said enough, but that you have said too much and too often.

If you have to keep repeating your point to make an impact, it may be time to stop talking.

4.7

Choose the right seat

No matter how well you are talking in your meeting, others will be affected by your body language. Use open body language and you will win more friends than with defensive body language. But where you sit also influences people's perceptions of what you have to say. Choose the right seat or you may not get the reception you want.

Be aware of personal space and territory in meetings. This varies from culture to culture and between genders. If you are having a meeting within your own company and country it should be relatively simple. If it is an international meeting, however, do your homework first. If you cross a personal space boundary accidentally by either sitting too close or in a seat that would normally be occupied by a senior member of the company, you are unlikely to have a successful meeting.

case study A friend of mine ran into some seating issues when he joined a major advertising company based in New York. He was unaware that territorial claims to certain seats had already been established in the meeting room. When he walked in for his first

There are a few rules to help you choose the right seat in most circumstances:

■ **Square tables.** On a square table, you will feel most cooperative with the person next to you and least with the person opposite you. The person on your right is more co-operative than the one on your left.
■ **Round tables.** These work well for meetings between people of equal status. However, if there is a mix of senior and junior people in the room, be aware that the same rules apply as for square tables.
■ **Long tables.** If you are on a long table and you have your back to the door you are not in a position of authority. If you want to be listened to, change positions and sit in the middle of the table.

The first time you go into a company meeting, check who likes to sit where.

meeting, fired up with ideas for a new account, he didn't consider where he sat. As the meeting progressed, though, it was clear he had 'taken' someone else's chair. He said it felt as if he had walked into their living room and sat in a favourite armchair.

Selling successfully

'People buy people' is the old saying. Of course, your product or service should be good but, even if it were great, you might still be unsuccessful if you have poor sales skills. So what are the secrets of selling successfully? Persuasive people develop genuinely positive relationships with their clients. They are friendly and open in their body language and make sure they are always in rapport. In other words, communication is key.

5.1

Be client-centred

The key to all the other secrets in this chapter starts with being client-centred. If your client doesn't think you are on their wavelength, they will pretty much dismiss everything you are saying right from the start of your sales pitch. If they think you are on their side, though, everything else is going to be easier.

So what do I mean by getting on the same wavelength? You will feel in tune with someone only when you have created a rapport. Remember to check out how the other person is sitting or standing; their posture and gestures too, as well as any particular way they have of speaking or words they frequently use.

Have you ever noticed how particular organizations use particular jargon or turns of phrase? If you pick up on these and use them at the same time as 'matching and mirroring' the other person's body

one minute wonder It's essential to discover what's important to the other person. What are their values and needs? So remember to ask questions such as: "How do you know when you have...?" and "What is it exactly you need from...?"

"If all my possessions were taken from me with one exception, I would choose to keep the power of speech, for by it I would soon regain all the rest" Daniel Webster, 19th-century American statesman

language, they will have the feeling that you belong in their environment. Nothing about you will feel out of place and they will be much more accepting of everything you say.

To be a successful seller you must ask questions:

■ **What?** Discover what a client needs specifically and also what's important to them as a business.
■ **Why?** Find out the other person's reasoning. Why they want what they want or need what they need.
■ **How?** Ascertain the way they do things in their organization and how they like things done by the people they work with.

Ask questions and listen (actively) to the answers. A persuasive person is always genuinely interested in others. They ask probing questions to find out what the key issues are and to weed out obstacles that might come up in the conversation.

Choose your questions carefully to become more persuasive and a successful salesperson

5.2

Show your client what's in it for them

In business you frequently need to sell either a product or service to an external client. You will sell most effectively if you spend time finding out your client's needs and what they really want. Here are some simple communication steps you can use to make sure you sell effectively every time.

Start off by establishing a rapport with your client. Then, if you follow the steps bulleted below, you can get your client to open up to you and tell you what's going to make them buy. This will make you far better at selling. The best thing about it is that the customer won't feel as if you are trying to force something upon them but simply that you want the best result for them.

■ **Home in on the outcome.** Ask what specifically does the customer or client want. What is their ideal? It could be a thing or a feeling.
■ **Examine the benefits.** What does this outcome mean to the potential buyer? When they have it, what will it be like? Will they feel a certain way? Look a certain way? Be able to be, do or have something?

one minute wonder Here is a simple set of questions to use if the client doesn't seem certain about buying. Firstly ask: "What would it take to convince you to think about buying this?" Then ask: "If we could find a satisfactory solution to this, would you be willing to buy?" This let's you know exactly what it will take to get the sale.

■ **Think about current and future situations.** When and where does the customer want it? Perhaps they have part of it already.

■ **Create a sense of expectation.** Does the customer know anyone who has one already? What does it do for them? Have they ever had something similar that they really liked? What did it give them? What did they see, hear or feel when they had it?

■ **Check the timing.** Ask yourself two questions: why does the client not have what they want already and is there anything that is stopping them having it now?

■ **Use the 'as if' scenario.** Focus on the outcome they want. Ask your client to see themselves as if they already owned the product: "Let's assume you already bought X. How did you know it was the right product to buy? How do you feel about it or see it? What told you it was a good decision?"

When people hear questions like this, what happens next is that they start imagining what it will be like to own the product.

Use the 'as if' model to get the client to try on the feeling of owning your product or service.

5.3

Win others' support

Whether you are a manager or simply a team member, you will need to sell your ideas at some point. Be enthusiastic, get the other people's attention and make sure you have lots of rapport when you talk. Selling ideas is easy. Follow these simple steps and you will make other people passionate about your ideas too.

If you want to advance in business, you need to get other people signing up to your ideas and supporting your goals. This means you will have to become a salesperson, whether you are formally one or not. Here are some steps that will make the difference:

■ **Grab the other person's attention.** Introduce the subject in such a way that it gets them interested. You can't assume they want to listen. Give them a reason to. Ask questions to confirm their interest level.

■ **Contextualize the idea.** Describe the context for the idea. Is there a problem to solve, for example, or a challenge to overcome?

■ **Focus on results.** Describe in as much detail as appropriate what result your idea will deliver. In other words, how will things be different in future? Describe the contrast with the current situation.

one minute wonder Paint an image of what the future will be like if your idea is accepted. Contrast this with a picture of what it will be like if they don't accept your idea. You want the client to experience in the moment the benefits they will derive from taking action now.

■ **Present your idea.** You have set the context to now describe the idea in detail. And, because you have set the context, the other person will be more receptive to your idea at this point.

■ **Stress the benefits.** Make sure that you maintain a rapport with the other person by checking their levels of interest. Describe the benefits to them, to the organization, the team and anyone else relevant.

■ **Counteract a negative response.** Think about the 'what ifs'. Suppose they don't adopt your idea? Talk to them about the negative consequences of not taking on your idea.

■ **Keep a check on progress.** Make sure you use open body language to keep the rapport going, and check their reaction by using open questions to draw out any issues.

■ **Get them on board.** Ask for commitment to action. What are the next steps? Outline the next steps needed to implement the idea, or ask them to suggest a first step.

Selling ideas is easy if you follow a step-by-step approach in the way you communicate.

5.4

Communicate credibly

Selling is about trust and credibility. No one is going to buy from a person who they think doesn't know anything about their product, doesn't believe in the product, doesn't look as if they want the best for you or is trying to bully or con you in some way.

Here are five steps to build credibility with your customer or client.

1 First of all, be congruent in everything you say. This means that your body language should be telling them the very same story as your words. Additionally, what you say on one occasion should be the same, or at least aligned with, what you say on every other occasion. If you are constantly changing your story or being contradictory in some other way, all your trust as a salesperson will be destroyed.

2 Once you have established congruency, think about your credibility. When you sell a product or an idea, you should always be prepared to be fair in how you describe it. Selling doesn't mean your product has to be perfect for your client to

"You don't have to be great to start, but you have to start to be great"

Zig Ziglar: American motivational writer

want to buy. It's the opposite to some extent. Only ever tell the buyer as much as they can believe about your product. If it's too mind-blowingly wonderful, suspicions will be raised.

3 Be prepared to describe what you see as the more limited or negative aspects of your product or service. As long as these are balanced by the more positive aspects, you needn't worry that this will make you vulnerable to losing a sale. All you are doing is building up credibility.

4 Then, when you do want to describe all the great features of what you are selling, be very specific. For example, tell your client they are not going to make an extra profit of 10% through efficiency savings but specifically an estimated 11.5%.

5 Finally, recognize that many clients do need some sort of external reference as evidence for either your credibility or your product's. Have referrals and documents ready for reference.

When you sell benefits, the key is to be specific and detailed.

5.5

Know why clients say "no"

There you are with your client, talking about what they want. You seem to be getting on very well – all the right things are being said. And yet, the client concludes the meeting or sales call with a line such as, "I will think about it", or "I have decided against it this time". What do you do next?

There are two basic reasons why people will not buy your products or services that can be countered quite easily. Once you have the skill, you should be able to talk your way around these blocks.

1 **Is it you?** The first reason clients say "no" is because they don't like or trust you. As this is down to you, this is easy to correct. Ask yourself how friendly are you being? Your words may be appropriate, but are you using open body language as well? Do you feel friendly? Perhaps you aren't establishing enough of a rapport? If you feel anxious or you don't like the client, they will be able to pick that up in your body language. Change the way you feel and they will change as well.

one minute wonder Use the 'Feel, Felt, Found' formula. These are great words for showing empathy and moving someone on beyond their initial resistance: "I understand how you feel. My previous client felt exactly the same at first. Now he's found he is saving money every month by using this service."

2 **Do they need it now?** The second reason is a lack of urgency. The buyer may like you and like what's on offer, and yet say something such as: "It sounds great, but I don't actually need what you are offering". Or perhaps: "I might need it at some point, but not right now". Or even: "I love it, but the thing is I don't have any money to buy it right now". How can you talk your client round, so that they genuinely feel a sense of urgency and want to make a decision to buy from you immediately?

Each time you hear a person say "I don't need this", they are really telling you that you haven't shown it to them in enough detail – the 'what's in it for me' factor. In other words, you haven't described the benefits of your product or service in a way that makes them want to have it more than they want to keep the money in their bank.

Find out the benefits for the customer and specifically the immediate needs they have. If you can show how your product will fulfil these needs, you will have a sale.

Check your rapport and give more detail about benefits if your client seems to be wavering.

5.6

Fire the imagination

What would it be like if you were lying in the most relaxing place in the world right now? Imagine what that would feel like. Now notice what happened when you started reading this. Using words that fire the imagination is a powerful way to get people thinking about the benefits your product will bring.

When you use words like "imagine" and "what would it be like if…", the listener does exactly what you ask. They really do think about the feeling or the image you mention. Any word that gets you to tap into the power of the imagination will have the same effect:

■ **Picture this.** "Picture what it would be like (if you had this car)." "What's it like when (you drive cars like this)?"
■ **Have you wondered.** "Have you ever wondered what it would be like (if you had this car)?"

---

case study A friend of mine called Dave works in car sales. I've occasionally had a chance to watch him operate, and he always says something like: "Imagine what it would be like if you owned this car." The potential buyer inevitably stops what they are doing and for

---

■ **Consider this.** "Consider what it would be like (if you had this car)." "What would happen if (you bought this car)."
■ **Just pretend.** "Just pretend for a moment (that you own this car)."

These words and phrases invite you to paint an imaginary future in your mind and, for the few seconds that you do this, it can feel very real. This is the same trick that hypnotists use to put people into a light trance-like state. In fact, it is so effective you had better be careful!

Why some salespeople fail is because they use power words by accident with negative images. For example: "I don't want you to imagine (the car will break down)". Then wonder why their buyers don't want to make a purchase.

So make sure you think before you use power words, and describe only positive futures with your words.

The imagination is one of the most powerful selling tools you have for winning over a client.

a few seconds tries out a future in their mind where they already own the car. It's almost impossible not to. And, if they like what they imagine, they are immediately much more open to what Dave says next and are a big step closer to buying.

5.7

Understand values

Can you remember the last time you saw an advertisement that really made you want to buy the product? Or can you think of a time when you bought something from someone? The chances are that the advert and the salesperson used 'values' to persuade you to buy.

What I mean by 'values' are the things that are really important to us. Now, of course, you and I are both unique and want very different things in our lives a lot of the time. But, having said that, there are some common ideas and ideals that most people value and want to attain across all countries and cultures.

If you use words that get people to think about these values when you describe the benefits of your product, they will become excited about what you have to say. This will make them much more open to buying the item or service you are describing with these words.

Here are some of the words that you can use:

new, proven, results, safe, free, best, improved, unique, value, save

one minute wonder You can soften how you sound by adding a little phrase at the beginning of your introduction, such as, "I am just wondering whether (you would like a car that is proven to save money". Or, "Just for conversation's sake...", or "I am curious as to whether...".

If you look around at newspapers and on radio and TV you may notice these words being used again and again. This is because they tap into universal ideas about getting something of particular worth that is special or the best on the market. As human beings, we like to buy things that show how special we are so we love things that give us a particular image.

This works even in business because we always need to justify our decisions to ourselves and others. It is easy to say that we had to buy the product because it was the best, or unique, or proven or safe. Somehow this makes our decision-making process feel safer.

Use these values words, together with your power words, for even more effect. For example: "Could you imagine what it would be like if you bought a car like this that was unique and could save you money on fuel? What would you feel like?"

Start using these words and phrases and notice how much more effective you become in sales.

Use 'value words' to get your clients to think about the benefits they will get from buying.

5.8

Avoid "but" and "try"

"It looks great on you but…", "I really loved what you did on that project but I think you could do something a bit different next time", "I will try to do it by Monday", "I will try to get there by nine, but I am not sure".

Every time you use the word "but" it destroys the positive words which go before it. You can state the most positive thing about someone and yet, as soon as you use the word "but" after it, the person listening immediately hears the whole sentence as negative.

The solution is to use the word "and" instead of "but". While "but" is a positivity destroyer, "and" is a positivity reinforcer. Look at these two sentences and you can see the difference.

- "That sounds great but I would like to get a discount."
- "That sounds great and I would like to get a discount."

Which sentence sounds more positive? It's the second that leaves the listener with a good feeling.

The word "try" is a similarly difficult word. Let's face it, if you hear someone say "try", what are your expectations? That they are going to do whatever it is to get the task done, or to not do it? Hear the difference between the following two sentences:

> **"**The shortest and the best way to make your fortune is to let people see clearly that it is in their interests to promote yours**"** **Jean de La Bruyère, French essayist**

- ■ "I am going to pick up that pen."
- ■ "I will try to pick up that pen."

The first one assures the listener that you believe that you can and will do it. The second sentence implies failure. You don't believe that you will want to, or be able to, pick up the pen.

If you are going to sell successfully, be careful with your language. As soon as you use "buts" and "trys", your client will start to doubt that you will fulfil your promises. They will be right to do so too, as, if you use that language, it is reflecting what is going on inside your brain. You probably have a few doubts and they show in your words.

If you catch yourself 'butting' and 'trying' all over the place:

- ■ Check what you really think about your product.
- ■ Check that you are happy about what you are offering the client.

Clear up your doubts and you clean up your communication.

Clean up your communication with yourself and your clients to make yourself more effective.

5.9

Don't think of a blue tree

Don't think of a blue tree. No, really, please don't think of a blue tree. Look, I told you not to. Don't let that picture of a blue tree come into your mind right now. Oops! Hands up, who is thinking of a blue tree?

So what happens if I tell you to that my product is "not rubbish" and "not expensive"? Yes, you'll probably wonder if it is rubbish and you'll certainly make at least a brief picture of it as expensive.

Create the right picture

Your brain thinks in pictures. If you use the right words it will make all the right pictures to help you sell your product. For example, this tree is beautifully green with lush leaves. When you walk close to the tree you will notice that there is a beautiful perfumed smell – the sweetest scent you have ever smelt.

What has happened? Your words have painted sensual images for your brain to pick up on. By using positive language these pictures are all enjoyable to experience.

one minute wonder Here's an additional idea you can use. What you want to show your client is very basic: "What you have presently, who you are presently, or how you feel presently are not satisfactory. You can do, have, or be more, and feel better." Use a variation on the latter sentence and you will always sell successfully.

Don't say what it's not

Use negatives and the brain has to make a picture of whatever you have described before trying to get rid of it. It doesn't hear the 'nots' and the don'ts'. It makes an image of whatever you are describing.

So there is no point saying, "don't think of a blue tree". If you don't want that image to go into your buyer's brain, don't create that image at all. Instead, you need to ask them to think of the image you do want them to imagine. For example, "please think of a green tree". Or, "my product is very good value and high quality".

Many people make the mistake of using negative language. Think of notices that say things like 'Don't Slip!'. What happens? Your brain makes a picture of you slipping. Far better to say 'Be Careful'.

As a brilliant sales communicator get rid of your negatives and pay attention to your language. Make sure you always use positive words to describe the positive qualities of your product.

Use positive language to make the right impression of what you are selling in the other person's mind.

5.10

Handle complaints flexibly

Hopefully, if you have flexible communication skills, you will never hear from the majority of your clients because you will have built trust with them. But, if someone isn't satisfied, you need to become an even better communicator. 95% of customers will do business with you again if you handle their complaint satisfactorily when they complain.

Customers often assume that, if they complain, the other person is going to be defensive or dismiss their complaint, so they get angry even before they start talking. Being defensive is the worst response to this. Instead, take these steps to reach a happy conclusion all round.

> **case study** Hiten says: "I used this strategy when a customer's TV had broken. I told him: "Since the problem seems to be in the wiring, the best thing would either be for me to send it back to the manufacturer for repair, which would take a few weeks, or give

■ **Build rapport.** First build a rapport with the customer. During the initial part of the conversation, let him talk for most of the time so that he can say everything he needs to. Show you are listening, though, by nodding your head and using eye contact. This will calm him down.

■ **Be empathetic.** Look for areas of agreement so you can use phrases such as "I understand why you feel…", "I agree…" or "I appreciate…".

■ **Check the details.** Then you can question to get all the specific facts and details of the complaint. Take notes if necessary. This will also assist the client to feel that you are taking the complaint seriously.

■ **Give feedback.** You need to feedback to the client what you think he is telling you. As you get the details, get agreement. Ask things like, "Have I got this down correctly?", "So this is what happened next. Is that right?" The client then knows that you have become an active problem solver on his behalf. Then you are ready to present a solution.

■ **Create a positive outcome.** Apologize if necessary, and lead the client to think about a positive outcome. Feedback the problem with an option about what you CAN do. At the end of your statement ask: "Since what has happened is…", "I would recommend that you do…", "If we do that, would that be okay?"

This concludes the conversation and everyone knows that they have got what they wanted.

Keep checking that you are dealing with a client's objections effectively.

you another TV now of a different make. I would recommend that I check which similar TVs we have and find one of the same quality. Would that be okay?" Because the complaint was dealt with straightaway, the client came back and became a regular customer.

Dealing at a distance

Technology has brought faster and more convenient forms of communication, and everything from phones to the Internet has helped give rise to flexible working and virtual contact. However, a lack of face-to-face communication also leads to opportunities for misunderstandings, as people often communicate in a far lazier fashion at a distance. This chapter gives you the secrets to maintain excellent levels of communication whatever the circumstances.

6.1

Be a flexible speaker

Telephones are a fast, convenient medium for business communication, but it is worth remembering that you are the voice of your business. Every time you speak on the phone, the other person will have either a negative or a positive image of the business, based purely on your words and your voice. Make sure you create the best impression you can.

Face-to-face, your body language carries about half your message to the person you are talking to. But, over the telephone, 85% of your communication comes from your voice: the speed with which you talk and the tone of voice in which you speak to someone. The actual words you say account for only around 15% of the message.

one minute wonder Notice where you normally breathe from as you speak. Chest breathing is shallow, Deeper breathing comes from the lower abdomen. The depth or shallowness of your breathing creates a different tone to your voice. Pay attention to how flexible you are in your breathing and, therefore, your speech.

Your goal when you talk over a phone should be to manage your communication through thinking about how quickly you speak as well as what you say. The average English speaker talks at about 150 words per minute. This sounds a lot, but luckily we can listen to far more than that – in fact 300 words per minute.

All very well, but nervous people amongst others tend to speed up their speech or 'eat their words'. This means that, without realizing it, they could be gabbling at up to 500 words per minute!

If you do gabble along too fast, you are immediately going to lose your impact and leave a negative impression the moment you start racing away because of your anxiety. The solution, though, is very simple. Follow these steps:

1   **Listen.** Each time you get on the phone, deliberately relax. Then slow down and listen to how the other person is talking.

2   **Pace.** Now check the pace of your voice. The most effective communicators pace their speech to match the speed at which the other person is talking.

3   **Smile.** Try smiling when you talk. Even though the listener can't see your body language, humans are so highly tuned to subtle differences that they will hear it in your voice.

Create a positive image over the phone by changing the pace of your voice.

6.2

Observe phone etiquette

Since you can't see the other person on the end of the line, it's easy to be casual on a telephone and not pay the same attention that you would if it were a face-to-face meeting. Poor communication over the phone will lose you customers, but pay attention to the basics of etiquette and you will see the impact.

Have you ever asked a caller to repeat themselves because you weren't paying attention? Or have they asked you to repeat yourself? Have you busied yourself doing something at the same time as you're talking because you know that the caller can't see you?

case study Sally is a salesperson who did relatively well at work but never got the top sales figures. She was sent on a leadership course and learnt to do voice warm-up exercises just like a professional actor. What she realized was that her voice had a huge impact on how effectively she sold to her clients, as the majority of her selling took place over the phone. By practising

If so, it's time to do something about your poor telephone etiquette. Here are some simple things that you can do to improve your telephone communication skills:

■ Focus on the listener. First of all, treat the person on the end of the phone as an individual by showing empathy and understanding.
■ Summarize. Repeat back messages and key details of the conversation to show that you are actively listening to what they say.
■ Do just one thing. When you're on the phone, just talk on the phone. Turn off your computer, put your book away and turn away from the TV. People can hear if you are painting your nails as you talk.
■ Check. Make sure the caller knows what you are going to do to follow up on the call. Ask: "Is there anything else I can do at this point?"

All this etiquette is lost, though, if it is said incongruently, or in a disinterested sounding voice. Your tone of voice 'leaks' clues to the listener, so pay attention to how you sound as well as what you say. Just as we know from facial expressions and movements of the body whether someone is listening attentively to us when we meet them face-to-face, we can pick up a lot from the other person's voice on the phone.

Show your interest in the other person by summarizing the key points of the conversation as you go.

deep breathing and warming up her voice every morning, she became much more confident as a telephone speaker. After a couple of months her sales figures also rose. Although it is difficult to say how much impact her voice had on her success, Sally is convinced that it has been an important factor, and she continues to use voice exercises.

6.3

Use emails thriftily

Emails are quick, efficient and convenient. They allow near instantaneous communication across the globe, not simply of text, but also of images and attachments. But there is a downside too: everybody's inboxes are getting fuller and fuller, and not all emails are essential to business.

Can you imagine not being able to send a picture or even a short video to a colleague in the office or in a different country? Communication has become so easy now that you don't even need to step away from your desk to keep in touch with anybody anywhere in the world.

Alongside this speed of communication, there's an informality which has tremendous benefits. It lets you reach people within different levels of an organization. In the past, you'd have had to set up meetings or write a letter. Now you can just send an email.

one minute wonder For each email, ask yourself: "Is this the best means of communication to use?" "Do I need to cc all these people?" "Would it be better to keep them in touch on a less detailed level?" "Is this essential for them to know, or just nice to know?"

"I believe that thrift is essential to well-ordered living"

John D. Rockefeller, American industrialist

Supposing you want someone in another country to have a first look at a draft document. You can send it quickly by email during the day and then follow up with one or two lines in the evening. If you are anxious for a reply, you can ask for an email receipt to make sure the reader has received it.

But there's a downside: too many emails. Then there's the 'cc' phenomenon, where some people seem to just cc emails to everybody in their company to give the impression that they're doing something by constantly sending and answering emails.

The problem is, it doesn't achieve real results. All this 'reply all' syndrome does is overburden your inbox and workload without achieving anything constructive or instructive.

It's great to keep people in touch with what you are doing, but, before you send your next email, STOP and THINK:

- Do you really need to send this person an email?
- Is this the best way for you to get your message across?
- If the answer is that you could just phone or talk to the person, then DO IT!

Imagine if every email you sent cost money. Would you send it? Be thrifty! Save emails!

Don't reply to the whole group if only one person needs your message.

6.4

Stay professional

The world is getting more casual. Some employees never write formal letters any more. They write emails for business and send texts in their private life. But the boundaries between what is appropriate for private and public communication can get blurred. Make sure you differentiate between what is appropriate communication within and outside business.

Emails aren't as formal as letters but they are permanent. Whatever you write is going to stay on the computer of the person who receives it until they delete it. A phone call just lasts for a few minutes but an email could last for weeks, months or years.

While you might get away with poor grammar, sloppy writing and half-formed thoughts in a text, an email in contrast does need to look more like a letter. Here are a few pointers:

one minute wonder Before you press 'send', always take time to re-read your email for unintended messages. If you were the person about to receive this, what might you think? Is there any room for misunderstanding in what you have written?

"You don't write because you want to say something; you write because you've got something to say" F. Scott Fitzgerald, American novelist

■ Get rid of exclamation marks and ellipses ('dot dot dots'). Proof-read and run a spell check.

■ Write a clear subject header, which shows the subject and purpose of the email.

■ Stick to business issues within the email. This means don't attempt to be funny unless you have a very close relationship with the recipient. Avoid sarcasm too, particularly if you are sending an email to someone from another culture. Remember, one person may understand what you have written very differently from another.

■ Be extremely careful about sharing personal gossip in emails and avoid criticizing other people in the organization. It is not appropriate in a business setting. From a practical point of view, think who your email could be immediately forwarded to. Would you want that to happen?

■ If you are angry, don't write an email. I'll say it again. Absolutely do not take out your anger by writing an email. You are not going to sort out anything. In fact, you are more likely to fuel the conflict. Why? Because the reader won't just read it once, but look at it again and again. What's more, they may misunderstand your words. When in doubt, take a big breath and go away and calm down.

Remember, if it isn't business, don't write it.

Don't write anything in an email that you wouldn't want sent to everyone within the company.

6.5

Don't use emails as avoidance

Some employees use emails as an avoidance mechanism. If you are afraid of your boss or are asked to do something you don't want to do, emails are a great excuse to get rid of problems. "If I send you an email I can avoid speaking to you" or "I can pass this problem on to you".

There are many difficult situations in which it is tempting to send an email rather than deal directly, face-to-face with another person. Here are a few examples:

■ **Disciplining an employee.** Should you send emails to discipline your employees or give negative feedback? Messages such as: "You're in trouble over this", "Your salary's being cut" or "You're sacked!". No! Absolutely not. Disciplinary messages need to be said in person.

■ **Dealing with personal matters.** If an employee is ill or has a personal problem, it is more appropriate and empathetic to talk to them directly. Email can come across as very insensitive and unfeeling.

■ **Ignoring problems.** Equally, you can't ignore emails to avoid, or put off, problems that need addressing. You can forget excuses such as,

"Writing is about communication, not how clever you are"

George Orwell, English novelist and essayist

"Oh sorry, I didn't do that because I never got your email", or "How strange! It must have got sent to the Spam folder". No one's going to believe you. Don't pretend you never received an email to avoid your manager when you think you have made a mistake.

■ **Avoiding conflict.** In business as elsewhere in life, many people hate conflict and will go to great lengths to avoid it. One recent survey showed that almost three-quarters of workers would prefer to send an email if they were faced with a potential conflict rather than have to deal with it by talking directly to the other person.

■ **Apologizing.** In the same survery it was found that, if they were called upon to say sorry for a mistake, they also found this easier to do by email. But, in both cases, emails shouldn't be used to avoid problems.

People think it's easier to send an email than look someone directly in the eyes if there's a problem. This is because somehow they feel they won't really have to take responsibility – that they are less involved. But it's inappropriate and won't do the person any good professionally in interpersonal issues inside the organization. An email may be fast and efficient, but that doesn't always make it appropriate.

If you choose to communicate in an email, ask yourself if this is the most professional method you could use. If you are at all in doubt, choose to talk directly to the other person.

Always check that sending an email is the most appropriate way to get your point across.

Ditching the difficulties

Business doesn't always run smoothly. We don't always like the jobs we do or the people we have to work with. What then are the secrets of getting on with people? How do you move from conflict and disagreement to building strong relationships? How do you share bad news? This chapter will let you into some of the communication secrets that will solve your difficulties.

7.1

Keep focused

If you know you are dealing with a difficult person and there could be problems, don't just lurch in and open your mouth. Always decide what is the best result you can get by communicating. Good communicators don't talk without a purpose. They have outcomes; a focus for the conversation.

If you have a difficult situation, before you start a conversation take a moment to ask yourself what result you want. This isn't just in difficult times, of course. Business people spend much of their day talking to colleagues, writing emails or making phone calls and generally being busy without really taking the time to work out what they want to gain out of their communications. They don't, therefore, consider which type of communication would be most effective.

one minute wonder Get yourself into a positive frame of mind before you start your conversation. If you show that you want to fulfil the needs of both of you, the other person is going to be more amenable to what you say from the start.

"Begin with the end in mind" Stephen R. Covey, motivational author

Stop and ask yourself these questions:
- "What do I want out of this interaction? What would be a win for me?"
- "What about the other person or people? What are they likely to want? What would be a win for them?"

These are very simple questions and yet not asked enough. Check to see if the result you want is possible. Would you be willing to settle for a lesser outcome if necessary?

Now, think about what are the major objections that might be raised by the other person. If there are likely problems or blocks, how can you overcome them?

Here are some things to think about:
- What problems might arise as a result of this interaction? How will you deal with each one?'
- Can you use any of the problems and turn them into benefits for the other person?
- How will you make sure that you have achieved the result you want by the end of the conversation?

This kind of planned communication is your best way to prevent problems and solve a difficult situation. Ideally, it should result in a win-win for everybody concerned in the interaction.

Always start communication by focusing on creating the outcome you really want.

7.2

Say "no" nicely

In business, it isn't enough to be nice and say "yes" all the time. You may win some friends but there is bound to come a time when you need to say "no", albeit nicely. If someone says, "do this for me" or "do you agree" and you can't say "no", you will end up doing things you don't want to and feeling resentful.

Difficulties often happen in business because one person is domineering or aggressive and they intimidate other people to go along with what they want. Many of us just give in and are passive because it seems the easiest way out in the short term.

If that sounds like you, it's time to learn to be assertive. These are some steps you can take which will make it easier to say no and yet still appear to be positive and cooperative with the other person.

one minute wonder Use your rapport skills. Match and mirror the other person's body language before you start speaking. If you do this, you'll feel better about what you say, and so will the other person. They'll feel more in tune with the message you want to get across.

"The art of leadership is saying no, not saying yes. It is very easy to say yes"

Tony Blair, former British prime minister

■ **Listening.** First of all, it is important that you stop and listen to what they are saying.

■ **Demonstrating.** Next, it's important to show you have listened. Acknowledge verbally that you have heard their request and that you are thinking about it.

■ **Being clear.** Now say what stops you from being able to help them in this situation. You can keep this both brief and quite general.

■ **Being positive.** Finally, leave with a positive statement so that the other person is left with a positive feeling. For example, you could do this by saying what an alternative for them might be, or what you might be able to help them with in the future.

Here's an example: "That sounds really interesting. Usually I would be happy to meet with that client for you. However, I have another commitment today. Perhaps you could ask Susan to do it instead. I would be happy to come with you another time."

By both starting your response with a positive and ending with a positive the other person feels understood and listened and the "no" feels polite rather than aggressive.

Learn to be assertive and say "no" positively to requests.

7.3

Control your emotions

The secret to communicating effectively in a potentially difficult situation is to control your emotions. If you get emotional, the other person will too. If you get angry, the other person will either feel angry or bullied. If you get upset, they may take pity on you but forever see you as pitiable. On a professional level, you don't want to get into these positions.

Whether you want to be assertive, deal with a complaint or break bad news, learning to control your emotional state makes all the difference to how the other person hears what you say. The more professional,

case study Every time Dan used to have a conversation with his boss, he would feel really nervous. His boss was intimidating: loud, extrovert, and he dominated the whole office. If he saw someone reading when he thought they should be selling, he would come up to them and tear the newspaper out of their hands. Over a month, though, Dan started changing his behaviour.

calm and rational you can be, the better you will come across in terms of what you want to say. All controlling your state takes is practice. Even if you are a highly emotional person, it's something you can do.

Each time you want to feel positive, use your memory and your imagination. It's a very simple but powerful technique.

■ **Breathing.** Pay attention to your breathing. Shallow breathing makes us more emotional. Calm your breathing down by taking a series of long, deep breaths.

■ **Positive thinking.** Try to recollect a time when you felt happy, confident, calm and relaxed. Imagine you are experiencing that right now. As you do, you will feel yourself experiencing positive emotions.

■ **Relaxing your body.** Now move around until your body feels really comfortable. Keep the body language of a happy, relaxed person and you will be happy and relaxed.

By remembering a time when you felt positive and imagining the scene as if it were happening to you right now, your body starts believing that it really is happening. Of course, you know you are just pretending, but, by pretending, you actually do change your emotional state.

By being able to control your emotions, you can also control the outcome of your communication.

He learnt to always come in looking and feeling confident. It was a pretence at first but in time became more natural. And gradually his boss's attitude to him changed. Rather than trying to bully him, his boss started stopping to chat. Dan came to realize that half of his boss's behaviour was bluff and bluster – it too had been something of an act.

7.4

Don't interrupt

Effective communication can't occur if you're constantly interrupting the person talking. Interrupting causes people to feel that they are not being listened to and valued. It can swiftly build up resentment. Resolve difficulties by not butting in.

Whenever you talk when someone else is talking, you disrupt the communication and cause a problem. It doesn't matter how well-intentioned you are, it stops good communication in its tracks. Whatever you're assuming the other person is going to say isn't necessarily what they are going to say.

Many people worry when they are about to have a conversation which they assume isn't going to be easy – for example, breaking bad news. They think the easiest way to control it is to do all the talking,

one minute wonder A technique mediators use to ensure effective communication when there is a dispute between two people is to wait when the person talking finishes their speech. They then ask the question, "Is there any more you want to add?", before giving ample time to think about this. Try this next time you have a tricky conversation.

> # "There cannot be greater rudeness than to interrupt another in the current of his discourse"

John Locke, 17th-century English philosopher

including interrupting if necessary. Actually this causes more problems. Even in a normal conversation it causes problems. These are some of the things people do when they interrupt:

■ **Bringing it back to you.** "Oh, I had a situation just like that" or "let me just tell you what happened to me".
■ **Finishing sentences for the other person.** "I know what you are trying to say" or "And then that happened didn't it".
■ **Making suggestions without listening.** "I really sympathize with what you are trying to say here, and I have an idea for you. You don't need to say any more." The speaker thinks they are listening, but they aren't really because they assume they know what is coming next.
■ **Other interruptions.** These may take the form of yawning, fidgeting, letting your mobile phone go off in the middle of a conversation, watching something or somebody else when talking or doing several things at the same time.

Stopping interruptions is a first step to really empathetic communication, and the best way to let the other person know you are interested in what they want to say. If you want to resolve a difficulty rather than cause a difficulty, stop interrupting and start listening.

You aren't being helpful by finishing sentences or giving ideas when someone else is speaking.

7.5

Challenge bad behaviour

If a person is causing you difficulties – getting angry or emotional, or simply doing something that is detrimental to the business – remember that their behaviour is not *who they are*. If you are going to communicate with them, focus on *what they are doing* rather than criticizing them as a person.

Labelling a person because of what they do or say is a very ineffective form of communication. It doesn't help to change behaviour. In fact, it may reinforce it, because the person feels misunderstood and may nurse a grievance as a result.

An 'is/ are' statement is a label. Here are some examples:

■ David has not finished the project in time, therefore he is lazy.
■ Melanie and Susan always come to work on time, so Melanie and Susan are wonderful people.

Labelling people is a lazy and subjective way of thinking and communicating. If you are saying nice things about someone, it doesn't matter too much. But if you are labelling someone negatively it does.

"It is human nature to think wisely and act foolishly"

Anatole France (1844–1924), French poet, journalist and novelist

Negative labelling will usually happen because you have observed another person appearing to do something that you don't like. It's easy just to say, "oh it's because they are such and such a person" rather than stand back and separate out what they are doing from who they are as a whole person.

Don't label them. Instead challenge the behaviour:

■ **Recognize human nature.** If you accept that we are all lazy, arrogant, difficult, great, wonderful, and everything else at different times, it is easier to draw back, deal with the actual problem and avoid labels.

■ **Speak specifically.** Tell the person what you have observed them doing and what effect it is having on you, other people or the business. This example concentrates on behaviour and is specific: "I noticed that you came into work an hour late today. When you are late in the mornings, I have to cover for you. This has a negative effect on me."

By commenting on the behaviour rather than the individual, the person you are communicating with is most likely to listen to what you say and actually change what they do.

When you point a finger at someone else, always remember that there may be others pointing back at you.

7.6

Listen empathetically

The deepest level of listening occurs when you hear the other person's point of view, and at the same time 'put yourself in their shoes' and imagine how they feel. This level of listening is very useful if you are coaching, negotiating, or giving and receiving feedback. It is a vital part of difficult conversations.

Empathetic listening can help you to build strong team relationships and defuse critical or conflict situations. Listening with empathy helps you to get a sense of what the other person is feeling even if you do not end up agreeing with them (and you certainly don't need to).

This listening skill may be about understanding another person's feelings, but it starts by you thinking.

case study Lily says: "I had never thought about empathetic listening until I went to a training session in which a group of us each told a short story about an unresolved issue. The other people in the group listened. First, we thought about how the story was being told: what words were used and its pace. Then we thought about what the person must be feeling as

■ **Think from their point of view.** As you begin the conversation, think about what the key issues in the situation are for the other speaker. Consider why they are talking to you about the issue and also what they want to hear from you in response.

■ **Pick up on their feelings.** If you are attentive to the clues in the conversation, you will find that you start to pick up their feelings. You may even be one step ahead of them, as many people are not self-aware enough to understand their own feelings.

■ **Work out the causes.** If successful, you will be able to work out, not only how the speaker feels, but also what that feeling is really about.

■ **Use your body language.** Show that you are interested and focused on the speaker. Be open, lean forward and then ask follow-up questions.

■ **Use effective phrases.** "I can see that...", "You must feel...", "I understand that...", "You sound very...". Make sure that you don't follow up with the word 'but', or you will undo all the good feelings.

Successful listening shows up in a feeling of warmth towards the other person, an indication of being in rapport. This is the best starting point for any difficult personal issue within a business environment.

Learn to listen empathetically, which means with the intention of understanding the other person.

they were speaking and telling different parts of the story. The final level was thinking about intention, and wondering what the person was going to do about the issue described. Finally we said what we had heard the story teller say and the story teller told us how accurate we were. It changed my view about two of the people, and overall I do listen much better now."

7.7

Be a great negotiator

Negotiating skills are vital to resolve big and small difficulties. Once you are an experienced negotiator, you will find yourself called on again and again within business to resolve misunderstandings that can otherwise escalate and cause real harm to business relationships and the bottom line.

The key thing in a negotiation is to begin with the objective of achieving a win-win situation – the outcome that is best for everyone. This means that you don't just respond to a proposal with a counter proposal, but you continually restate what has been said and raise questions to find out what the real outcome is behind each proposal.

case study Tom says: "The one thing I have learnt in negotiations and tricky conversations is to speak only for yourself. When you use a statement starting with the word 'I', you own that statement. When you say 'we' or 'you', you speak on behalf of others and assume what their views will be. I have found that making assumptions is a big mistake in negotiations, as it

"Failure is the foundation of success" Laozi, Chinese sage

■ **Find out each person's objectives.** You need to know what each participant in the negotiation wants and needs. They may be different.

■ **Probe and clarify for meaning.** People use words as facts. Are you sure you understand what they mean? Question to make sure.

■ **Summarize.** Restate what has been said to increase understanding and test arguments as you go: "Let me be sure I know where we are now".

■ **Communicate your feelings.** Do this through phrases such as, "I am having trouble with this part of the issue", "I get the feeling that we're not talking about this point enough".

■ **Avoid attack.** If you are attacked, check what outcome the other person has in mind to deduce the reason for attacking you.

■ **Take breaks.** If you are getting stuck, stop what you are doing or take a break. Having some space can resolve a lot.

■ **Look for a 'win-win'.** Generate at least three options for a way forward. Choose the best and go with it.

Test for understanding throughout a negotiation.

leaves lots of room for misunderstandings. Using 'you' can also sound aggressive or accusing, whereas 'I' is just speaking my opinion as I see it. When you are engaged in a dispute, using 'I' separates feelings from facts. I now use language like, "I am having trouble understanding this", rather than, "You're not making yourself clear"."

7.8

Avoid judgement

"Well I think that argument's rubbish", "Yes I know that's what you want, but it's not as important as what I want", "That's such a ridiculous thing to say". If you are as judgemental as this in your communications, you aren't going to get very far in business or in social life. So what should you do?

Avoiding judgement means not making remarks which devalue the other person. It also means not thinking these things either. Why? Because, if you don't value the other person and their needs, you will never really go for win-win solutions.

A situation in which two or more people have different viewpoints and different needs can very easily develop into a conflict. On a big scale, all you need do to see this is look around the world and see all the conflicts that are caused by different attitudes and thinking. Conflict can escalate out of the smallest difference, if each person obstinately stands their ground and doesn't try to find a way out.

You may not be able to end up agreeing on everything, but you can end up coming to a satisfactory compromise if you negotiate and communicate compassionately.

The idea of 'non-violent or compassionate communication' was developed by the American psychologist Marshall Rosenberg and is used successfully worldwide in the most difficult communication situations. Key to this is that you suspend judgement about the person you are negotiating with. If you judge them, they will know it.

Here are the basic points to remember:

■ **Suspend judgement and avoid coercion.** Creating fear, guilt, shame, punishment or even reward through your judgement simply doesn't work in the long term to resolve a conflict situation. But when you suspend judgement, you avoid trying to bully or coerce anyone to do what you want them to do. This is the first step to resolution.
■ **Show empathy.** By suspending judgement, you'll be able to find a connection between you and the other person. You do this by showing empathy, which encourages the other person to feel secure.
■ **Encourage them to open up.** When the person picks up that you are really interested in what they have to say, you are more likely to get to the heart of what they really want, as they will feel safe to open up. Then you can carry on with the negotiation.

Show you are genuinely open to hear what the other person wants to say.

Jargon buster

Active listening
Listening with full participation of the listener, as opposed to passive hearing.

Auditory
Another word for the hearing sense.

Body language
Non-verbal communication. How you communicate through the voice and body.

BOOST model
A model for giving feedback to others.

Chunk size
The amount of detail a person likes to process in one go (global/ specific).

Compassionate communication
See non-violent communication.

DEAL model
A model used in negotiations.

Kinesthetic
Another word for the feeling sense.

Matching and mirroring
The techniques of copying another's body language and/or speech patterns, which produces feelings of rapport.

Myers Briggs
A well-regarded psychometric type indicator. In other words, a way of assessing and categorizing people, based on their psychological preferences.

Neuro-linguistic programming
Often known just as NLP, this is a popular methodology, or set of techniques, about communication and goals.

Non-violent communication
A mediation and communication style developed by American psychologist Marshall Rosenberg.

Outcome
The result or desired and specific goal.

Pacing and leading
A technique for changing feelings of rapport in a group.

Personal zone
The invisible territory or personal space surrounding a person.

Rapport
The sense of trust and feeling of acceptance and friendliness generated between two or more people.

Reframing
A technique used to put a different perspective on a given situation.

Representational system
A preferred communication style.

Sandwich model
A model for feedback and alternative to the
BOOST system.

Straddle
A sitting or standing position which can
denote power in a relationship.

Summarizing
The technique of restating what has been
agreed, used particularly in negotiations.

'Towards' and 'away from' motivation
Positive and negative values that motivate
people in all situations.

Values
That which is important to you in any
given situation.

Visual
Another word for the seeing sense.

Further reading

Adair, John *Effective Communication:
The Most Important Management Skill of All*
(Pan Books, 2009) ISBN 978-0330504263

Alder, Harry *Handbook of NLP:
A Manual for Professional Communicators*
(Gower, 2002) ISBN 978-0566083891

Back, Ken and Kate *Assertiveness at Work: A
Practical Guide to Handling Awkward Situations* (McGraw-Hill Professional, 2005)
ISBN 978-0077114282

Barker, Alan *Improve Your Communication
Skills: Creating Success* (Kogan Page, 2006)
ISBN 978-0749448226

Boyes, Carolyn *Need to Know? Body
Language* (Harper Collins, 2005)
ISBN 978-0007205943

Boyes, Carolyn *Need to Know? Neuro-
Linguistic Programming* (Harper Collins,
2006) ISBN 978-0007216550

Covey, Stephen R. *7 Habits of Highly Effective People* (Fireside: Workbook edition,
2004) ISBN 978-0743250979

Covey Steven R. *Principle Centred leadership*
(Simon and Shuster, 1992)
ISBN 978-0671711160

Etherington, Bob *Selling Skills for Complete
Amateurs* (Marshall Cavendish, 2008)
ISBN 978-1905736454

Goleman, Daniel *Emotional Intelligence:
Why it Can Matter More Than IQ*
(Bantam, 1995) ASIN B0018P1SGQ

Goleman, Daniel *Working with Emotional
Intelligence* (Bantam, 2000) ISBN 978-
0553378580

Harvard Business School Publishing
Harvard Business Essentials: Negotiation
(Harvard Business School Publishing,
2003) ISBN 978-1591391111

Hargie, Owen *The Handbook of
Communication Skills* (Routledge, 2006)
ISBN 978-0415359115

Hindle, Tim *Negotiating Skills – Essential
Managers* (Dorling Kindersley, 1998)
ISBN 978-0751305319

Jago, Wendy; McDermott, Ian
The NLP Coach (Piatkus Books, 2002)
ISBN 978-0749922771

Kiersey, David and Bates, Marilyn *Please
Understand Me: Character and Temperament
Types* (Prometheus Nemesis, 1984)
ISBN 978-0960695409

Knight, Sue *NLP at Work: The Difference that Makes a Difference in Business* (Nicholas Brealey, 2002) ISBN 978-1857880700

Kratz, Abby and Dennis *Effective Listening Skills* (McGraw-Hill: Business Skills Express Series, 1995) ASIN: B001G4418Q

Paterson, Randy J. *The Assertiveness Workbook: How to Express Your Ideas and Stand Up for Yourself at Work and in Relationships* (New Harbinger Publications, 2000) ISBN 978-1572242098

Rosenberg, Marshall B. *Nonviolent Communication: a Language of Life* (Puddledancer Press, 2003) ISBN 978-1892005038

Rosenberg, Marshall B. *Surprising Purpose of Anger: Beyond Anger Management, Finding the Gift* (Puddledancer Press, 2005) ISBN 978-1892005151

Sharpe, Robert *Assert Yourself* (Kogan Page, 1989) ISBN 978-1850917809

Tracy, Brian *Advanced Selling Strategies: The Proven System of Sales Ideas, Methods and Techniques Used by Top Salespeople Everywhere* (Simon & Schuster, 1996) ISBN 978-0684824741

Useful websites

www.anlp.org

The Association for Neuro-Linguistic Programming provides details of NLP training providers, programmes worldwide and other related NLP information. Membership required.

www.ppimk.com

NLP resource for businesses and the wider community.

Communication **secrets**

www.BusinessSecrets.net